FORGOTTEN YOUTH

Undocumented Immigrant Youth

Stephen Currie

ReferencePoint Press®

San Diego, CA

© 2017 ReferencePoint Press, Inc.
Printed in the United States

For more information, contact:
ReferencePoint Press, Inc.
PO Box 27779
San Diego, CA 92198
www. ReferencePointPress.com

LIBRARY OF CONGRESS CATALOGING-IN-PUBLICATION DATA

Names: Currie, Stephen, 1960- author.
Title: Undocumented immigrant youth / by Stephen Currie.
Description: San Diego, CA : ReferencePoint Press, Inc., 2016. | Series:
  Forgotten youth | Audience: Grade 9 to 12. | Includes bibliographical
  references and index.
Identifiers: LCCN 2016011961 (print) | LCCN 2016016881 (ebook) | ISBN
  9781601529800 (hardback) | ISBN 9781601529817 (eBook)
Subjects: LCSH: Immigrant youth--United States--Social conditions. | Illegal
  aliens--United States--Juvenile literature. | United States--Emigration
  and immigration--Juvenile literature.
Classification: LCC JV6600 .C87 2016 (print) | LCC JV6600 (ebook) | DDC
  305.235086/9120973--dc23
LC record available at https://lccn.loc.gov/2016011961

Contents

Introduction

Youths Without Papers

In the early 2000s an impoverished single mother named Lidia Rodriguez decided to move her family from Mexico to the United States. Lidia, however, lacked a green card—a document giving foreigners legal permission to live and work in the United States—and did not believe she would be able to get one; the United States issues only a limited number of these cards, and demand for them is high. Instead, Lidia paid a so-called coyote, a guide who smuggles people across Mexico's border with the United States, to bring Lidia and her three-year-old daughter, Mariana, into Arizona. "We were running at night in the desert," Mariana says today, repeating the stories her mother told her about the trek. "We were really tired but some guys carried me on their back."[1] The two successfully reached the Phoenix area, where Lidia found a job. Later, she sent for her other children, who had remained in Mexico with relatives.

Lidia and her children were undocumented immigrants—people who lack the proper papers to live and work in the United States. In particular, she did not have a Social Security number, which people must have in order to hold a legal job. Nonetheless, Lidia made up a Social Security number and used it to get work. When Mariana turned fifteen, though, her mother became ill and was unable to work regularly. To keep the family going, Mariana used a fraudulent Social Security card and a fake US birth certificate—purchased for her on the black market by an aunt—to get a job in a sandwich shop. For two years Mariana worked nearly forty hours a week while maintaining a full load of courses in high school. But one day in 2012, when Mariana was a high school senior, state law enforcement officers arrested her for being in the country illegally. Mariana eventually spent several months in detention centers and was nearly deported—sent back to Mexico—before being allowed to return to her family.

Stories like Mariana's are common among undocumented children and teenagers in the United States. Like Mariana, many undocumented youths (though by no means all) come from Mexico. Like Mariana, many arrived here by crossing a border without being detected. And like Mariana, many undocumented youths in the United States come to recognize that they cannot participate fully in American life. In Mariana's case, that realization came when she needed false documentation to apply for a job. For other unauthorized young people, the watershed event has to do with getting a driver's license, applying to college, or joining the military. Sooner or later, most undocumented teenagers recognize that they cannot easily take part in the rituals of adolescence that their native-born peers take for granted.

Fear and Detention

Mariana's story also illustrates a second reality faced by most undocumented teenagers: fear of being caught by US authorities. Mariana knew that her immigration status might be discovered at any moment. A hostile neighbor, a vindictive teacher, a suspicious boss—any of them might report Mariana and her family to immigration authorities if they knew that she was here illegally. Moreover, Mariana knew she needed to keep herself out of any possible trouble. Even a small infraction—such as riding a bicycle after dark without lights— could bring her to the attention of the police, who might discover while questioning her that she was not a legal resident. "My mom had always been scared of [police] officers," Mariana says, "and I got that fear from her."[2] Hundreds of thousands of other undocumented teenagers over the years have experienced this same type of anxiety and dread. This constant state of fear also

> "My mom had always been scared of [police] officers, and I got that fear from her."[2]
>
> —Undocumented teenager Mariana Rodriguez.

Women and children who illegally crossed the US-Mexico border await processing at a temporary detention facility in Arizona. Most will be sent back to Mexico.

helps define what it is like for undocumented youth to live illegally in this country.

Finally, though Mariana was not deported, she came very close to being returned to Mexico, perhaps forever. A significant percentage of undocumented children and teenagers in the United States—no one knows exactly how many—are deported each year. Others, like Mariana, may not be deported but are held in detention centers, where they may experience loneliness, verbal abuse, and a complete lack of privacy. As is frequently the case with teenagers facing deportation, moreover, Mariana had left her birth country when she was so young that she no longer had clear memories of living there. She knew little of Mexican customs and was unacquainted with her Mexican relatives. For many undocumented teenagers, the possibility of being deported does not imply returning to friends and family in a familiar country; rather, it means starting over in a strange land.

The constant fear of being found out, the inability to share in typical American experiences, and the grim realities of detention and deportation all combine to make the experience of being an undocumented youth in America very different indeed from the experience of being a legal immigrant or a US citizen. As Mariana's case demonstrates, undocumented children and teenagers face challenges and complications unknown to those whose right to live in America is unquestioned. Being an undocumented youth is to live in a shadowy, secretive, and occasionally shameful world in which options are limited, immigration status is rarely discussed, and the freedoms and rights extended as a matter of course to native-born Americans do not necessarily apply. Living in this way is difficult. But as Mariana and others like her demonstrate, it is by no means impossible.

Chapter 1

Undocumented Immigrants

The United States has often been called a nation of immigrants. Its original government was founded by people whose ancestors largely came from Great Britain, and during the nineteenth and twentieth centuries waves of migrants from countries such as Ireland, Poland, Mexico, the Philippines, and Russia came to settle within US boundaries. Some, especially from countries such as China and Italy, soon returned to their home countries permanently. Many more quickly put down roots in the United States. Indeed, America soon became known across the world for its diversity of cultures. Today, except for a very small number of people who are descended solely from Native Americans, every American has ancestors who came here in the last few centuries—and often much more recently than that.

High levels of immigration to the United States continue today. Each year approximately 1 million immigrants are given official permits to move here. Just as in earlier times, the great majority stay. This steady flow of immigrants gives the United States the most immigrants of any country in the world by far. As of early 2016, close to 40 million people in the United States were documented immigrants—that is, they had papers officially entitling them to live and work in this country. Russia, which ranks second for the number of immigrants, is home to just 11 million immigrants. And the desire to enter the United States remains high among people from other countries. A 2012 survey suggested that perhaps 140 million people around the world, amounting to nearly half the current US population, would move to America if they could.

Most of these 140 million people never bother to apply for admission to the United States. Still, the demand for immigration permits far exceeds the available supply. With the odds against them, many foreign nationals decide not to wait for official permission to enter the United States; instead, they arrive illegally. Some are hoping for a better economic future; the United States has a significantly higher standard of living, after all, than many other nations. Others are hoping to escape religious or political intolerance (and sometimes violence) in their home countries. In either case, they are willing to break the country's immigration laws in order to obtain residency in the United States. By some estimates, currently about 11 million noncitizen residents of the United States do not have documentation. Known by a variety of terms, including *undocumented immigrants* and *unauthorized aliens*, they are living in the United States illegally.

Most undocumented immigrants to the United States are adults. It is adults, after all, who are best able to travel, adults who have the resources to move to a new country, and adults who are most likely to find full-time work once they arrive in America. But quite a few of these adults are part of family groups that include children and teenagers. Thus, the population of the United States at any given time includes hundreds of thousands of young people who are here without the proper documentation. In some ways undocumented youth, especially teenagers who have been living here for years, are much the same as Americans who were born in this country. In other, less obvious ways, however, the experiences of undocumented youth are wildly different from those of native-born Americans and legal immigrants. On a regular basis, this population deals with challenges and complications unknown to the great majority of Americans.

Numbers and Locations

It is difficult to determine the exact number of undocumented youth currently living in the United States. Since undocumented aliens are here illegally, most do not willingly reveal their status to such government figures as census takers, school officials, or police officers. Because making an accurate count is impossible, demographers must estimate the number of undocumented youth residing in the United States. Not surprisingly, estimates vary widely. Some experts believe there are fewer than 1 million undocumented minors in the United States, but others think the true figure is more than 2 million. Most researchers accept that about 1.5 million people under the age of eighteen are living in the United States without proper permission. But no one knows how accurate that number actually is.

Where these undocumented youths live is easier to determine. Experts generally assume that undocumented minors are distributed across America in numbers more or less similar to undocumented aliens overall. Since more than half of all unauthorized immigrants live in just six states—California, Texas, Florida, New York, New Jersey, and Illinois—the same is probably true of undocumented minors. Southwestern states such as Nevada and Arizona also have sizable undocumented populations and therefore large numbers of undocumented minors as well. In Nevada, for instance, an estimated 8 percent of the population is there illegally—the largest percentage in the country. But every state has at least some immigrants who have crossed the border illegally. Even Vermont, West Virginia, and Maine—small states with little ethnic and racial diversity—are each home to perhaps a thousand young people who lack documentation.

People who study immigration also have a good idea of where the undocumented population comes from. Most unauthorized immigrants, though certainly not all, come to the United States from developing nations. Close to half of all undocumented aliens are from Mexico. Another quarter of the total comes from various other countries in Latin America, mainly Central American nations such as Honduras and El Salvador. Asia accounts for about one in ten undocumented aliens, a figure that has been growing in recent years, with many of these migrants coming from China, India, or South Korea. Most of the remaining 15 percent of undocumented aliens are Canadians and Europeans, with a small number coming from Africa and Oceania. In general, experts believe that these proportions roughly describe the origins of unauthorized minors in addition to unauthorized adults. Thus, just as undocumented young people live in every US state, the home countries of unauthorized children and teenagers represent all regions of the world.

Immigrant Population by State

This map shows the approximate distribution of undocumented aliens by state, according to information gathered by Pew Research. These numbers are estimates, but the figures given are believed to be within about 5 percent of the actual numbers. Studies of where undocumented people live do not typically sort out the population according to age, making it even harder to know exactly where young undocumented aliens live. However, experts generally accept that unauthorized immigrants under eighteen are distributed across the US in about the same way as the undocumented population overall. States with high numbers of undocumented immigrants, then, probably also have high numbers of undocumented children and youth.

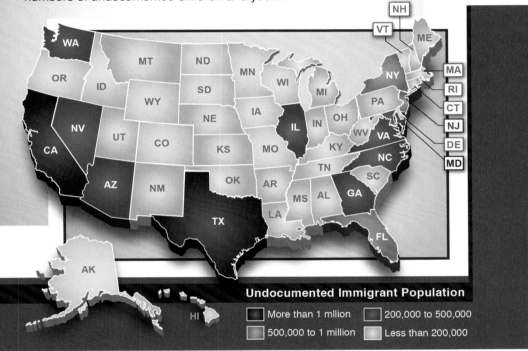

Undocumented Immigrant Population

☐ More than 1 mllion ☐ 200,000 to 500,000
☐ 500,000 to 1 million ☐ Less than 200,000

Source: Jeffrey S. Passel and D'Vera Cohn, "Hispanic Trends, Chapter 1: State Unauthorized Immigrant Populations," Pew Research Center, November 28, 2014. www.pewhispanic.org.

Overstayed Visas

Regardless of where they live today, undocumented families—including teenagers and children—use two main methods of entering the United States. The first method, used by a majority of undocumented immigrants from outside the Americas, involves entering the United States legally. Foreign nationals who wish to enter the United States temporarily can usually obtain a document called a visa. This document permits entrance into the United States for a definite purpose and for a specified length of time. A tourist visa, for example, entitles the bearer to spend up to six months traveling within the United States. Student visas, similarly, allow holders to enter the country for educational reasons; in 2015, more than a million foreigners were enrolled in American colleges and universities. And business visas allow employers to bring foreign workers into the country for a limited period.

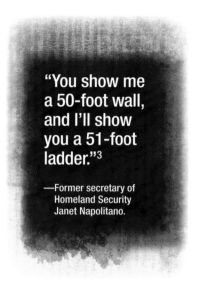

"You show me a 50-foot wall, and I'll show you a 51-foot ladder."[3]

—Former secretary of Homeland Security Janet Napolitano.

The great majority of people traveling on visas return home when their documentation expires. But some do not. Instead, they find jobs and housing and remain in the United States hoping to evade detection. When adults enter the country on a visa, the documentation often extends to their minor children as well; thus, plenty of youths arrive in the United States as legal, if temporary, visitors. By some estimates, 40 percent of all undocumented aliens today initially arrived in this country with a legitimate visa that they later allowed to expire. Immigration officials consider these people to have *overstayed* their visas. Overstaying a visa is considered a serious offense by American immigration officials, especially once the visa is six months or more out of date. Those who are caught can usually expect deportation.

Border Crossers

The second method of illegally entering the United States does not involve a visa. Instead, it consists of crossing a border without being detected. The United States has nearly 6,000 miles (9,656 km) of land borders with Mexico to the south and Canada to the north. For most of their lengths, these borders are either completely unguarded or only lightly patrolled; the border cuts through desert, prairie, and mountainous regions, and migrants can often hurry across these sections on foot without being detected. Even where the border follows a river, determined migrants can find a way to cross. The Rio Grande, one of the West's longest rivers, delineates the boundary between Texas and Mexico, for example. But where the Rio Grande is shallow, people wade across; where it is deeper and faster, they have been known to cross the river on rafts.

In an effort to cut down on the number of people crossing into the United States illegally, the US government has constructed fences and walls along some sections of the border with Mexico. These barriers, however, have frequently failed to do the job they were meant to do. Would-be migrants have used pickaxes and shovels to tunnel beneath fences and walls. Nor is building a high wall particularly effective. As former secretary of Homeland Security Janet Napolitano puts it, "You show me a 50-foot [15.2 m] wall, and I'll show you a 51-foot [15.5 m] ladder."[3] Some migrants are smuggled across the border in the trunks of cars or are concealed in the backs of trucks driven by US citizens or people

Braving waist-high water, two people wade across the Rio Grande. The river, which marks the boundary between Texas and Mexico, is a well-known route for undocumented immigrants who are trying to enter the United States.

with the proper papers—an easy way to enter the United States if border guards do not perform a thorough check of the vehicle.

Whether climbing ladders, hiding in car trunks, or wading across a river by night, crossing the border illegally is a common way of reaching the United States. Experts estimate that as many as 3 million people try to enter the United States via this method each year, most coming across the border with Mexico. This number is widely believed to be less than it was before about 2008, when the US economy was better than it is today. Still, even this figure represents three times the entire number of legal immigrants allowed to settle in the United States each year. Perhaps 400,000 of these border crossers are caught by American authorities as they try to make their way into the country, but the rest evade detection. As with those who enter the country on visas, entire families often attempt to cross the border without proper documentation.

Different Journeys

The two methods of entering the country differ in important ways. Though remaining in the United States after the expiration of a visa can result in legal action, simply entering the country with appropriate papers is easy and relatively worry-free. Immigration officials at US airports look closely at a family's documentation to make sure it is legitimate. Fraudulent identity papers can be purchased on the black market in a number of nations, but the vast majority of families will be waved through checkpoints with few questions asked. Even if a child's parents already plan to overstay their visa, they rarely communicate this information to their dependents. Thus, the children believe they are simply taking a vacation or moving to the United States temporarily while a parent takes a new job. The dominant emotion experienced by most youth who enter on a visa, then, is excitement.

That is emphatically not the case for those who try to make their way undetected across a border. There is no way to suggest to a child or a teenager that sneaking across a border in this way is either legal or safe. Climbing a ladder, even at night and

Farmworker Children

The American agricultural industry employs several million people known as migrant workers. The great majority of these men, women, and children are foreign-born. Most come from Mexico and Central America, and they are here on a seasonal basis. During harvest time they travel from one farm to another, picking fruit and vegetable crops such as apples, grapes, onions, and lettuce. Once the harvest is over, they usually return to their home countries. Many of these workers have legal permission to be in the country. Many others, however, do not.

Though men make up the bulk of migrant workers, quite a few migrants travel in family groups, with parents and their children often working side by side in the fields. By some estimates, as many as half a million migrant workers in any given year are under the age of eighteen, with some being as young as twelve. They work long hours for little pay, performing the same repetitive tasks all day long; they are exposed to pesticides, labor in hazardous weather conditions, and work with heavy farm equipment that can cause severe injury. Housing, provided by their employers, often consists of tents, shacks, or broken-down trailers. Medical care is difficult to find, poverty is rampant, and the traveling lifestyle makes it difficult for migrant children to attend school on a regular basis. It is never easy to be an undocumented child or teenager in the United States, but being an undocumented farmworker under eighteen is especially difficult.

in a sparsely populated area, is dangerous. The tunnels running below border walls can be alarming, especially to a child. Running across a boundary line or rafting across a border river is nerve-racking at best and terrifying at worst, especially as there is always the possibility that US border officials will be waiting on the American side of the line, ready to send the migrants back to where they came from. And children being smuggled into the country in a vehicle are warned to stay extremely quiet—or risk discovery and possible detention for every passenger.

For many of these migrants, moreover, the act of crossing the border is only one part of a long and difficult trek. Migrants bound for Arizona or parts of Texas, in particular, often must walk miles through the Mexican desert before even managing to reach the border. The desert conditions are harsh, with brutal heat during the day and cold temperatures at night, and finding the way can sometimes be difficult. In addition, many of these would-be immigrants are carrying insufficient food, clothing, and water. Should they manage to cross onto US soil, undocumented aliens still must continue through the desert until they can reach the towns and cities that represent their destinations—this time with the added burden of watching out for immigration police. "Our journey took days," reports one Mexican boy, now living in Arkansas, who crossed the border in this way at the age of seven. "We marched on, moving mostly by night, weighed down by worries, bags, and younger siblings."[4]

Innocent Victims

Regardless of how they arrived in the United States, young immigrants without documentation did not generally make the decision to leave their homeland for a new country. Their parents were choosing to seek a new life elsewhere, and the children, naturally enough, came too. "I didn't choose to come here," points out one undocumented teenager. "I was 8 years old. How is an 8-year-old going to say to her parents, 'No, I can't go. I don't want to go.' If I stayed there, who was I going to stay with?"[5] From a moral point of view, advocates for undocumented youth argue, children who came to the United States before late adolescence should be held blameless for being here without legal permission. Bronwen Anders, a pediatrician and advocate for undocumented children, has referred to undocumented youth as "the innocent victims of illegal immigration."[6]

But though everyone agrees that undocumented children did not intend to break the law, the American legal system makes no distinction between them and their undocumented parents. Simply by virtue of being in the United States without documentation, these children are guilty of criminal behavior. If they are caught, they are subject to detention and deportation. Those accused of being here illegally can try to prove that their papers are indeed in order.

"We marched on, moving mostly by night, weighed down by worries, bags, and younger siblings."[4]

—A Mexican-born boy who crossed the border into to the United States.

17

The DREAM Act

The Development, Relief, and Education for Alien Minors (DREAM) Act was originally proposed in 2001 by US senators Orrin Hatch and Dick Durbin. Its purpose is to give legal status to young undocumented immigrants who have spent much of their life in the United States, are clearly committed to the country, and have skills that can benefit America. The provisions have been slightly modified over time, but in essence the proposed legislation offers a path to permanent residency to long-term undocumented immigrants who came to the United States before turning sixteen, have served in the military or attended college, and have no criminal record.

Supporters believe the DREAM Act is fair to immigrants and good for America. They point out that the legislation would be especially beneficial to those immigrants who came here when they were young, as they often have no true home country to which to return. They also argue that the United States needs and wants capable, loyal residents, no matter where they come from.

Opponents of the DREAM Act, however, have a very different point of view. They believe that the legislation would set a bad precedent by rewarding those who entered the country illegally. Their concerns have held up passage of the DREAM Act. Though the legislation, in one form or another, has been brought to Congress several times since 2001, and though President Barack Obama has been a supporter of the bill, the DREAM Act has yet to pass.

Alternatively, they can argue that there are extenuating circumstances, most notably that they are fleeing political or religious oppression in their homelands. And indeed, some detainees may ultimately be allowed to stay in the United States on these grounds. But demonstrating oppression is not easy. The burden of proof is on the detainees, and American courts typically rule against them.

Whether they arrived by plane or concealed in the back of a flatbed truck, whether they overstayed a visa or never had one to begin with, whether they arrived at the age of ten months or ten years, undocumented youth in the United States experience fear, anxiety, and a sense of separation from their peers and the rest of society. Afraid of attracting notice, they often avoid activities and experiences that their native-born counterparts take for granted. The legal system, similarly, denies them rights that legal immigrants enjoy, and detention and possible deportation are always possibilities. Fearful of being caught, barred from participating in many aspects of American life, and always wondering if deportation is in their future, undocumented teenagers frequently describe themselves as "growing up in the shadows"[7]—and it is easy to understand why.

Chapter 2

Fear

For undocumented immigrants under the age of eighteen, living in the United States can be a frightening experience. Any moment, at least in theory, could bring a knock on the door from immigration officials demanding to see a family's papers. Any day could bring a difficult call from the local police, or a series of uncomfortable questions from a guidance counselor or an assistant principal. With some justification, undocumented youth worry that events such as these are likely to end in only one way: with arrest, detention, and eventual deportation. Elioenai Santos, a Mexican national living in California, is just one of many who learned this lesson at an early age. Santos recalls his uncle saying that "every undocumented person has to be prepared for the worst."[8]

The fear experienced by undocumented youth, however, is not simply about the prospect of being caught and returned to another country. It is also about ambiguity. By the time adolescence begins, undocumented young people generally understand what it means to be in the United States illegally and just how insecure their futures are. Many increasingly realize that they are being consigned to a life on the edge of society—Americans in culture and education but not Americans where the government or the law is concerned. "Being undocumented means instability, uncertainty," says an undocumented graduate student. "You have no future. You can't plan. You can't envision what you want to do. You feel locked in a box. And it's hard to come to terms with the fact that you're going to be like this for you don't know how many years."[9] Being afraid, then, becomes a way of life.

Indeed, the fear experienced by undocumented youth can guide how they live their lives. Many undocumented minors do their best to avoid situations in which they might attract the attention of law enforcement officials—or anyone else who might learn the truth about their immigration status and pass it on to authorities. This behavior, while reasonable, comes at enormous cost. Again and again, undocumented youth try to stay out of the limelight. Some hang back in school, getting grades below their capabilities so they will not stand out. Most hide their history from everyone around them, even from close friends and well-meaning adults, because they fear that no one can be trusted with the truth about their immigration status. In the process, they often hide more than just their status; they hide important parts of themselves as well.

The result is unsurprising: many undocumented youths find it difficult, if not impossible, to relax fully and enjoy their lives. That uncertainty, that insecurity, is always present. For some, it lurks just below the surface. For others, it is a constant companion. As a high school student identified as Paulina puts it, "I am always afraid. . . . I am walking down the street or wherever I am, and I am completely aware of myself, to make sure that I am not

Young people who are in the United States without permission constantly worry about their secret getting out. They understand that they could face deportation—as this young woman is—if anyone learns of their status.

doing anything I am not supposed to . . . being responsible for everything that I do. Making sure I am not doing anything at all. And I'm just afraid. I am afraid."[10] Paulina's fear is an experience common to virtually all undocumented young people growing up in the United States today.

Fear in Childhood

The overwhelming sensation of fear experienced by many undocumented youths can begin very early in life. In some families, children are told when they are quite young—sometimes even before they begin school—that the family is in the country illegally. These children are cautioned to keep their immigration status a secret from everyone, including friends, neighbors, and school personnel. That caution invariably leads to suspicion—and sometimes to a deeply rooted fear—of the rest of the world. Jose Arreola, born in Mexico but raised in the United States, was always scared that something bad could happen to his family. Even at the age of five, he worried almost constantly that his parents would be deported while he was out of the house. "He didn't understand who would take his parents away or why," a reporter writes, "but he went to school every day fearing that he would never see them again."[11]

Arreola's fears are far from rare among children who are in the country illegally. Social worker and author Luis H. Zayas writes about Virginia, a six-year-old in Missouri whose father, a Mexican national, cautioned her not to give away any information about her parents' lack of documentation. The child, Zayas writes, took the warning more seriously than her father had intended. Though she spoke freely at home, Virginia decided it was safer not to open her mouth at all while she was in preschool and kindergarten. "She was extremely timid," Zayas reports, "and would not talk with anyone, including the bilingual teacher who was brought in to work with her."[12] The fear of giving away the family secret was so great that Virginia could not make friends, connect with teachers, or engage in learning the way a young child should.

Research, moreover, bears out the depth of the dread felt by even very young children. Sociologist Joanna Dreby, for example, has found that many undocumented children have "intense

Fear, Anxiety, and Mental Health

The effects of fear on undocumented youth can be significant. In 2008 researchers at the University of North Carolina investigated the mental health of Latino adolescents in the state. The great majority of the teenagers in the study were undocumented. The study found that 18 percent of the teenagers showed signs of depression, a higher rate than for the population as a whole, and 31 percent—nearly a third—had signs of anxiety, again higher than the general population. Researchers also determined that just 4 percent of their subjects had ever gotten mental health services. Other studies have arrived at similar results.

For many mental health specialists, these findings are not a surprise. It makes sense to them that people who live their lives in a state of fear would develop mental health issues such as anxiety and depression. "Feeling insecure and uncertain about your life and your future has serious mental health consequences," says Josefina Alvarez, a professor with a particular interest in mental health issues among Latinos. "Feeling stigmatized and unwanted can also have a negative impact on self-esteem and may lead to depression and other negative behaviors."

Worse, Alvarez points out, even those undocumented teenagers and children who get mental health benefits may not receive exactly the interventions they need. The undocumented population, she explains, often has different needs from the general public. "In the absence of training," she says, "most of us are not prepared to work effectively with immigrant groups."

Quoted in Kris Anne Bonifacio, "Undocumented Youth Struggle with Anxiety, Depression," Youth Project, January 25, 2013. www.chicago-bureau.org.

fears"[13] of raids and deportations. Dreby writes of a boy who admonished his little brother to sit up straight in his car seat when the police drove past the family vehicle, just in case the officer might be tempted to stop them for a car seat infraction. Dreby also describes the life of a young child who made plans to run away in the event that the police showed up at his home to ask for his family's papers. These children, and others like them, fear constantly for the safety of their family.

And when those fears are confirmed, as they are when a family member is arrested or deported, the child's mental health can be at serious risk. Dreby describes the case of a six-year-old boy who experienced terrible nightmares following the deportation of his father. At one point the child had a breakdown at school. "He was screaming and yelling that his dad killed his mother,"[14] Dreby writes. For this child, the stress and the fear of trying to live a normal life in a distinctly abnormal situation proved to be too much. "The fear of deportation and the uncertainty of living in the shadows," writes a reporter, "can likely cause and exacerbate serious mental health problems for immigrant families."[15] This includes young children.

Secrecy and Truth

Though young undocumented children may indeed feel exceptional fear, most do not develop this degree of anxiety this early in their lives. The main reason is that parents often do not tell their young children the truth about their immigration status. In part, that is to keep the children from always feeling afraid. It is an effort to give their children as normal a life as possible. There is also a practical reason for not revealing the family's legal status to a child: a child who does not know the truth cannot accidentally blurt out the family's true status to a stranger, an immigration officer, or the police. Keeping the truth from children for this reason is easy to understand.

But the deception cannot last. Eventually even the most sheltered teenager learns the truth. Jose Antonio Vargas, born in the Philippines, came to the United States as a small boy and moved in with his grandparents, who were naturalized American citizens. Vargas believed he was in the United States legally; he even had his own green card to prove his legal status. But when he turned sixteen, Vargas went to apply for a driver's license. "When I handed the clerk my green card as proof of U.S. residency," Vargas writes, "she flipped it around, examining it. 'This is fake,' she whispered. 'Don't come back here again.'"[16] It turned out that Vargas's grandfather had purchased a falsified card for his grandson. For over a decade Vargas's grandparents had concealed the truth from him, hoping to spare him from the fear of knowing he could be deported at any time. In the end, though, they could not prevent that fear. They could only postpone it.

Still, it is unusual for undocumented youth to discover their status as late as Vargas did—and unusual for them to discover the truth in such a dramatic way. Much more common is for children to hear the truth directly from their parents when they are between the ages of about ten and fourteen. But however undocumented teenagers and children learn the truth, the majority are aware of their status by the time they begin high school, and nearly all the rest learn the truth within a year or so after that. Virtually all unauthorized immigrants, then, learn to experience fear before they turn eighteen—and many learn it long before.

Fear and the Police

The fear experienced by undocumented youth can be intense, even crushing. Elioenai Santos, unable to obtain a driver's license because of his unauthorized status, generally relied on family and friends to give him rides. Occasionally he drove a borrowed vehicle despite not having the legal right to do so. While driving someone else's car one day, Santos was pulled over by a police officer. He was worried about the possibility of getting a traffic ticket, of course, but what terrified him was the threat of being deported. "I felt like my heart stopped," Santos told a journalist. "I was in a fog. I was confused, scared." In the end, Santos got away with only a warning—and an instruction to call someone who could drive the car home—but the incident shook him deeply. "Living like that," he concludes, "is a problem."[17]

For many undocumented youths, teenagers in particular, fear is connected most

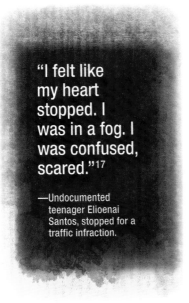

"I felt like my heart stopped. I was in a fog. I was confused, scared."[17]

—Undocumented teenager Elioenai Santos, stopped for a traffic infraction.

specifically to people in authority. "We're so afraid of the people who are supposed to be helping us," says Viridiana Hernandez, a Mexican national who came to Arizona as a baby. The sight of a police car, the arrival at school or home of an immigration agent — these situations can alarm undocumented teenagers or children who wonder if this might mean the end of life in the United States. Hernandez vividly recalls a time when the sheriff of her county declared a crackdown on unauthorized aliens, sending law enforcement officers into the streets to seek out people with no legal right to be in America. "Parents stopped taking their kids to school," she says. "My family was afraid to go out."[18]

Fear of an encounter with US Immigration and Customs Enforcement (ICE) agents colors every aspect of life for young undocumented immigrants. Parents often teach their children to trust no one because they believe that anyone can be a potential informant.

Misinformation about the reach of the government, moreover, goes unchallenged among many undocumented families. Mohammad Abdollahi moved at the age of three from Iran to Michigan. As a teenager, he learned from his mother that the family had overstayed their visa and were in the country without documentation. She also explained that the federal government was considering a piece of legislation known as the DREAM Act, which would potentially allow Abdollahi to remain in the country as a legal resident. "But don't look it up on the Internet," she instructed him, "because surely the government will find out and come after you."[19] Abdollahi, more aware than his mother of the limitations of government, looked it up anyway. But his experience indicates the degree to which fear of government in all its forms permeates the daily lives of undocumented immigrants, youth and adults alike.

> "We're so afraid of the people who are supposed to be helping us."[18]
>
> —Arizona resident and Mexican native Viridiana Hernandez.

For some undocumented families, indeed, fear of government officials pervades virtually every aspect of life. The most dreaded agents belong to Immigration and Customs Enforcement (ICE), often known simply as Immigration. This organization is responsible for finding, arresting, and deporting people here illegally. In the eyes of undocumented aliens, ICE is to be avoided at all costs. It is rumored to have extraordinary power: an enormous number of agents and a broad network of informants. The result can be near-constant anxiety about being captured by officers from ICE, a fear that adults frequently pass on to their children. Arizona resident Alma Rodriguez, Mexican by birth, recalls that she rarely went anywhere when she was a child. "Dad was scared to take us anywhere," Rodriguez recalls. "He knew Immigration was all over the place. . . . We were always home."[20]

Friends and Strangers

Fear is not limited to government officials and police officers. Many undocumented aliens have at least some anxiety about all

27

"Out of the Shadows"

Most undocumented immigrants, regardless of age, do their best to stay hidden. They try not to draw attention to themselves for fear that they will catch the eye of ICE or another law enforcement agency. But some undocumented youths have chosen a very different path. They have decided to proclaim their immigration status as a form of protest against what they see as unfair laws against the undocumented—and as a way of coming "out of the shadows."

The movement, which began with a rally in Chicago early in 2010, has always been led by young adults. The people who make up this movement have engaged in plenty of political protest. They have staged sit-ins at government offices, have gotten themselves arrested at the US border with Mexico, and have held rallies at which movement leaders publicize the fact that they are undocumented.

These tactics have caused some consternation among some supporters of the undocumented—particularly among the parents and grandparents of the protesters. "Oh my God, what are you doing?" one woman asked her daughter after a protest march in New York City. "Are you trying to get us deported?" Some worry that the greater attention focused on the protesters will backfire, especially in places where anti-immigrant sentiment is high and government officials may see a political advantage in arresting and deporting leaders of the movement. To date, however, that result has not been common. As of 2016, the protests were, if anything, gaining in strength and intensity.

Quoted in Helen O'Neill, "Teenage Undocumented Immigrants Coming out of the Shadows," *Huffington Post*, May 20, 2012. www.huffingtonpost.com.

strangers—along with acquaintances such as fellow students, teachers, coworkers, and neighbors. Even friendly, helpful people might actually be ICE informants, ready to turn an unwitting family over to Immigration if they let their illegal status slip. And if anybody can be a danger, at least in theory, then it makes sense to trust nobody. Ana Maria, a Brazilian high school student living in

Massachusetts, was tempted to confide her immigration status to her guidance counselor—but changed her mind at the last moment. "Who knows who she might tell?"[21] Ana Maria wondered. Zessna Garcia, a Mexican national and a resident of Arkansas, also kept the truth to herself. "No one in my high school knew I was undocumented,"[22] she says.

The fear of being found out affects children's relationships with their peers, especially in schools and neighborhoods where most children were born in the United States. Viridiana Hernandez knew from early on that she was a Mexican citizen, but she was instructed not to share this information with anyone. "I always would say I was born in Phoenix," she recalls about her childhood. "One day at school, some kids started saying, 'I was born in this hospital. Oh, I was born in that one,' and I thought, 'Uh-oh.' I didn't know what to say, so I changed the subject."[23] Hernandez was fortunate; she was able to shift the discussion so that no one learned her secret.

At a rally in New York City, a sixteen-year-old youth wears a T-shirt that proclaims: "Undocumented, Unafraid, Unapologetic." He spoke these same words to the crowd that had gathered for the "Coming Out of the Shadows" rally.

In the same way, undocumented high school students often avoid certain types of activities because of their fear of arrest and deportation. "There's safety in not being noticed,"[24] concludes a website describing life among undocumented teenagers and children. Even being out with friends is tricky. For a high school student who is an American citizen, committing a relatively minor offense such as underage drinking, petty vandalism, or fist-fighting may carry few significant consequences. The same offenses committed by an undocumented immigrant, on the other hand, can lead to deportation. "As long as I live a pretty safe, not-too-rowdy life, I can be okay," says Zessna Garcia. "You have to be careful when you go out . . . trying not to break the laws, not do anything small . . . so you won't get a police officer to look at you or question your status."[25]

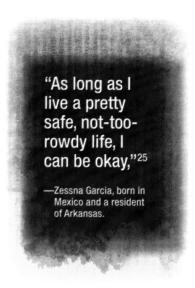

"As long as I live a pretty safe, not-too-rowdy life, I can be okay,"[25]

—Zessna Garcia, born in Mexico and a resident of Arkansas.

For the great majority of undocumented youth, then, fear is always present. It guides what they do; it shapes who they are. Being in the United States illegally, writes Jose Antonio Vargas, means "going about my day in fear of being found out. It means rarely trusting people, even those closest to me, with who I really am."[26] In one way or another, this fear marks every aspect of an undocumented youth's life. Indeed, many of the young people who are fighting to obtain rights for people in the United States illegally have adopted as their slogan the Spanish phrase "Sin Papeles, Sin Miedo"—or, in English, "Undocumented, Unafraid."[27] For these young immigrants, the goal is to step out of the shadows and into the light, and to live their lives without fear.

Chapter 3

Rites of Passage

As teenagers move toward adulthood, they experience a number of milestones, or rites of passage, that mark their progress along the way. For many, getting a driver's license is one such milestone. So is applying for a summer job or part-time employment after school. Many students who are involved in music look forward to going to choral or band competitions in distant cities; high school foreign-language classes sometimes travel to other countries during school breaks. Events such as a homecoming dance or senior prom can represent milestones as well. And the end of the high school years are marked, for many students, by college applications or plans to join the military. Not every American high school student reaches or cares about each of these milestones, but the majority of students take part eagerly in most of these.

For undocumented teenagers, however, the situation is different. While some of these rites of passage are available to people who are here illegally, most are not. The complex legalities of their situation can make it impossible for unauthorized students to leave the country with a student tour group, for example—and if they did manage to leave the United States, they would have no guarantee of being readmitted. Getting a legitimate job requires a Social Security number or a green card, both of which are unavailable to undocumented aliens. Some states do offer driver's licenses to undocumented aliens who meet certain requirements; the majority of states, however, do not. And though laws generally do not prohibit undocumented immigrants from attending college, filling out applications is a waste of time for many teenagers in this situation. Undocumented students cannot benefit from in-state tuition discounts at most state colleges and universities, and they

Participating in the traditional rituals of teen life can be difficult for undocumented youth. Even a trip with a high school band can be off-limits to a young person who does not have any form of legal identification.

are ineligible for government-backed student loans. Without these benefits, college is typically too expensive.

Some of the difficulties faced by undocumented youth in this regard may seem trivial, and in a sense a few of them are. Compared to the constant fear of being deported, for example, the troubles caused by the inability to go on a field trip with a school orchestra are minor. But some of the rites of passage missed by undocumented teenagers are much more significant than a school trip. The impossibility of legally getting a job prevents these young people from earning money, for example, and since many undocumented families are poor, that can be a significant hardship. The inability to find a job also prevents undocumented students from gaining valuable work experience. And keeping otherwise well-qualified high school students from attending college can severely dampen their career prospects and lifetime earning potential. Viewed in this light, preventing undocumented aliens from participating in American rites of passage does have major consequences.

But even if the only rites of passage were field trips and the like, the inability of undocumented teenagers to participate completely in ordinary teenage life would still lead to a sense of disconnection from the rest of society. Undocumented teenagers watch their native-born and naturalized peers get their driver's licenses, find after-school employment, and begin the process of applying to colleges, knowing full well that they cannot do the same. Some teenagers in this position lie out of embarrassment, telling curious friends that they have no interest in learning to drive or explaining that they cannot look for a job because they have to concentrate on their studies. Others are up-front about their reasons for not taking part. In either case, undocumented high school students frequently experience feelings of loss and separation stemming from their exclusion from activities and privileges that other American high school students take for granted.

Trips and Licenses

Not being able to take part in special school activities is one way in which undocumented high school students miss out on common rites of passage. Travel with school groups—especially international travel—is a frequent stumbling block. Philippine-born Jose Antonio Vargas, who sang in a choir in his California high school, heard from his choir director that she was considering taking the singers on a tour of Japan. Unwilling at first to reveal his lack of documentation, Vargas explained that he would be unable to go on the trip because of money. His family could not afford the cost, he said. The choir director told Vargas that they might be able to find him some financial help, whereupon Vargas told her the truth. "I can't get the right passport," he said. "I'm not supposed to be here."[28] Rather than touring Japan without Vargas, the choir director changed her plans and took the choir to Hawaii instead—a trip that Vargas was able to join.

"I can't get the right passport. I'm not supposed to be here."[28]

—Jose Antonio Vargas, an undocumented California resident, to his school's choir director.

Not all such stories have a positive ending. Other students do not trust school personnel enough to tell them their undocumented status. Nor are all teachers as willing as Vargas's choir director to change plans to accommodate the needs of an unauthorized student. Many students simply say they cannot go, whether because of money or some other reason, and no one tries to talk them out of it. Yves Gomes, born in India and brought to Maryland at the age of fourteen months, is one example. Though Gomes, an excellent student, took many French classes in school, he stayed home when the rest of his class went on a trip to France. Even domestic travel can be difficult if students lack proper identification. A Colorado student identified as Michelle hoped to accompany her eighth-grade class on a trip to Washington, DC. The students were to fly to their destination, however, and Michelle's parents believed that her Mexican identity papers, which Michelle would need to show at the airport, might mark her as undocumented. In the end, Michelle stayed home.

"I couldn't share in my friends' joy of getting a driver's license."[29]

—Luis, an undocumented college student from Mexico.

Being kept out of a school trip may sadden or anger an undocumented student, but other indignities are worse. Perhaps the complaint heard most often among undocumented students has to do with being denied a driver's license. As of early 2016, twelve states, including California, Illinois, and Colorado, issued licenses to at least some unauthorized immigrants. This list, moreover, has grown considerably in the last few years: before 2013, only four states offered undocumented residents the chance to get a license. But even today many undocumented aliens in these twelve states do not qualify for a license. Several of these states require paperwork such as income tax returns, which not all undocumented immigrants have. And those twelve states notwithstanding, undocumented aliens still cannot legally obtain a license to drive in about three-fourths of the country.

Independence and Dates

That can be problematic for many teenagers. Getting a license is an important rite of passage for countless young people, and undocumented teenagers who do not have this opportunity feel left out. "I couldn't share in my friends' joy of getting a driver's license,"[29] remembers Luis, a college student from Mexico. For some undocumented teenagers, this inability to obtain a license

The Driver's License Debate

Few debates regarding undocumented aliens are as intense as the question of whether people in this population should be eligible for a driver's license. Immigrant rights groups argue that giving licenses to the undocumented does plenty of good and very little harm. They point out that cars are a necessity for working and living in many parts of the country; the reality, they say, is that undocumented immigrants need to drive and will drive whether they have a license or not. Ensuring that unauthorized immigrants can get licenses, in this view, improves safety on the roads. Others argue that denying licenses to undocumented aliens simply encourages them to buy forged licenses on the black market. And still others point to the issues faced by undocumented teenagers and others whose lack of a license makes it hard for them to participate in all aspects of American life.

Opponents take a very different perspective. They argue that it is unwise to give unauthorized aliens any documentation that legitimizes their presence in the United States. Opponents would prefer to keep undocumented aliens from becoming part of American society, and they see a driver's license as a step toward integrating them into the United States culturally and politically. They also worry that offering a driver's license will encourage more undocumented aliens to come to the United States. Finally, they argue that giving licenses to undocumented immigrants presents a security issue. Licenses, in this view, could allow potential terrorists to establish residency in the United States and move about the country more freely.

makes them realize just how different they are from the people around them. "It was hard," recalls California resident Alondra Esquivel, whose high school friends got licenses—and often cars as well—when they turned sixteen. "I felt left out. They were able to do things, go places, and I couldn't."[30]

The lack of a license impacts other rites of passage as well, most notably dating. Cars have been at the center of dating activity for many years. Stereotypically, at least, the boy is supposed to drive to the girl's house to pick her up for the date, but that is obviously impossible for boys without licenses. For some undocumented aliens, the impact on dating is perhaps the worst aspect of being unable to drive. "When [I] ask a girl on a date, I can't pick her up," says Rodrigo, a Brazilian immigrant living in Massachusetts. "That's what sucks the most, when I think about it."[31] As an advocate for undocumented aliens points out, most teenagers find the idea of taking the subway to the high school prom to be distinctly unromantic. For those without licenses, though, there may be no other choice.

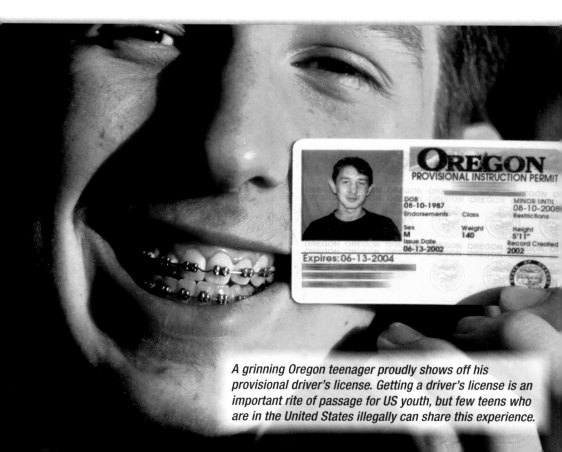

A grinning Oregon teenager proudly shows off his provisional driver's license. Getting a driver's license is an important rite of passage for US youth, but few teens who are in the United States illegally can share this experience.

More generally, the issue of driver's licenses is important because students without licenses have little independence. Some large cities, such as New York, Washington, and Chicago, have extensive public transportation systems, but even in these communities it can be difficult to travel efficiently between certain neighborhoods via bus or train. Smaller cities typically have much more rudimentary public transportation, and rural areas often lack any public transportation options. To get to school, work, or elsewhere, undocumented teenagers must rely on rides from friends, neighbors, and family members who are here legally. In the case of Arely Gonzalez, a Mexican national living in Arizona, that sometimes meant being chauffeured around by her younger sister, who qualified for a license by virtue of having been born in the United States. For Gonzalez, having to rely on a younger sibling for rides was embarrassing—but it was also necessary.

Finding Work

Obtaining a driver's license is one milestone; for many students, getting a job is another. More than 3 million high school students in the United States work after school or during the summer, according to the US Census Bureau; that represents more than one-fourth of the high school population. But applying for a job in the United States requires a Social Security number—and these are issued only to citizens, legal immigrants, and foreign nationals temporarily in the country for job-related purposes. Because they cannot obtain a Social Security card, undocumented young people cannot legally find work. While their peers accept jobs in fast-food restaurants, convenience stores, and summer camps, undocumented teenagers are once again forced to the sidelines.

As with driver's licenses, this inability to get a job is problematic because of how it impacts the teenager's sense of belonging and self-worth. It also presents a practical issue. Most undocumented families are poor and could use the extra income of a part-time job to help make ends meet. The lack of a Social Security card, then, affects the family financially. The need for another wage earner, especially in single-parent households, sometimes pushes young people to buy forged Social Security cards on the

37

black market. Using a fraudulent card is a crime, however, and the risks are great. Other undocumented teenagers find work in the underground economy, where jobs are informal and income is unreported. Some find work cleaning houses for cash, for example. These jobs, however, pay little in comparison to legitimate jobs. They also may not provide steady or consistent hours, and they carry no legal protections for workers.

The lack of legitimate jobs is also an issue because it denies students valuable work experience. Even the most menial of positions at a chain restaurant provides lessons in teamwork, punctuality, and following directions. Some jobs, moreover, are stepping-stones to more interesting work later on. As a high school student, Dan-el Padilla Peralta was invited to apply for a full-time summer job working as an adviser to younger students. Padilla, born in the Dominican Republic, would be paid for his work. Just as important, the job would teach him about working with other advisers, being a mentor, and more. Padilla applied and was accepted. But when his new employers discovered that he did not have a Social Security card, they rescinded the job offer. In the end, Padilla was allowed to work as a volunteer adviser without pay. Though he regretted the loss of income, he was glad to have the work experience. Most undocumented teenagers are not so fortunate.

College and Beyond

The realization that jobs and driver's licenses are unavailable to them usually hits undocumented teenagers when they are fifteen or sixteen. Within a year or so, many of them are grappling with yet another rite of passage in which they often cannot participate: going to college. Though the lack of documentation does not generally preclude unauthorized students from attending college, guidance counselors at many high schools dissuade those without Social Security numbers from even bothering to apply. "I thought that I could go to college," says a Brazilian immigrant known as Jessica. "But once it came down to sit down, talk to the counselor, the first thing they asked was, what my Social Security [number] was. And I didn't have one to put on the applica-

For many teens high school graduation represents a time to plan for a job or college and career. These options are not available to many undocumented immigrant youths, who struggle to find their place in society.

tion. So they all said the same thing 'You can't go, you can't go. You can't do it.'"[32]

Many colleges actually do accept students who lack Social Security numbers. The bigger issue for many undocumented students is coming up with the money to pay for college. State

"I Breathe American Air"

Undocumented youth who come to the United States as young children often grow up thinking of themselves as American. This is one of the reasons why learning their true immigration status can be deeply distressing for some young people. These young people often emphasize their Americanness in efforts to get politicians to lift some of the barriers—such as restrictions on driving, federal funding for college, and job possibilities—that prevent undocumented immigrants from fully taking part in American society. "People say, go back to your country, but where are we supposed to go?" asks one young woman. "This IS our home, the one we pledged allegiance to every morning before school." In the words of Alaa Mukahhal, who was born in Kuwait but was raised mostly in Chicago,

> I breathe American air, travel on American roads, eat American food, listen to American radio, watch American TV, dress in American clothing. I have attended private and public American schools, read American authors, was taught by American teachers, speak with an American accent, passionately debate American politics and use American idioms and expressions. A piece of paper cannot define me. I am a Muslim, an Arab, a Palestinian and an American.

Quoted in Helen O'Neill, "Teenage Undocumented Immigrants Coming out of the Shadows," *Huffington Post*, May 20, 2012. www.huffingtonpost.com.

colleges and universities have two tiers of tuition charges—one for students who reside outside the state boundaries and a heavily discounted price for students living in the state. In most states, however, undocumented immigrants do not qualify for the in-state discount, forcing them to pay much higher tuition charges than their neighbors who are legally in the United States. Nor are unauthorized immigrants permitted to take out federal student loans, a major source of college funds for legal residents. It is sometimes possible to get private scholarships or loans, but in the majority of states, college is economically out of reach for much of the undocumented population.

The recognition that college is not a possibility is devastating for some students. These young men and women worked hard in school, spent time studying, earned excellent grades, and saw college as the logical next step in their lives. Many were planning on careers such as nursing, engineering, or teaching, for which a college degree is a requirement. Now their dreams are being denied—and in a way that once again separates them from their peers. "I cried and cried; I couldn't stop," a young woman recalls about her reaction the day she understood that college was out of the question. "At school, all my friends talked about it, all excited. They talked about what colleges they wanted to go to, what applications they had sent already, and they asked me where I was applying." Like many others, this girl could not bring herself to tell her friends the truth. "I said I hadn't decided yet."[33]

Not all high school students are college bound, of course, but similar issues cloud the lives of undocumented teenagers who are seeking other career paths. Those hoping to move directly into the job market are disappointed; like part-time employment for a teenager, full-time employment for an adult requires a Social Security number. Joining the military is not generally an option either. A young woman known as Cristina had a slightly older friend who had enlisted in the army and was enjoying her experience. "She told me about it," Cristina explained to an interviewer. "They seemed to be paying for her college. She was traveling. I wanted to travel."[34] Cristina was bitterly disappointed when she learned that her immigration status would prevent her from following in her friend's footsteps.

"I cried and cried; I couldn't stop."[33]

—An undocumented student upon learning that she could not go to college.

For undocumented teenagers, then, life in America is a series of missed milestones. While their friends go on class trips, they stay home; while their peers earn driving privileges, they take the bus. Dating can be difficult, and getting a legitimate job impossible. And the excitement and drama of applying to colleges or enlisting in the military is inaccessible to most undocumented teenagers. The cost of missing out on these rites of passage can be huge. Undocumented students feel left out by their social groups and separated from the rest of society. They lose out on experiences that other students take for granted; they cannot advance their education and careers in the same way as their peers. Missing these milestones, then, is at once an indignity and a barrier to full participation in American life.

Chapter 4

Detention

The fear of being deported is perhaps the greatest worry of undocumented young people, and it is not difficult to see why. People who are deported are sent back to their home countries and are forbidden to reenter the United States for a period of at least ten years. Those who are deported lose their friends, their schools, and, often, the only homes they know—in some cases, forever. Worse, deportation can split families, with an undocumented mother and son, say, being returned to another country while a father who is a legal immigrant and a younger daughter born in the United States are permitted to stay. For undocumented youth who came here at a young age, the prospect of going to the country of their birth is especially troublesome since they often have no memory of living there and are unfamiliar with the culture, customs, and even the language. Being deported, in these situations, means learning to survive in a very different society.

The process of deportation can begin in several different ways. Sometimes law enforcement officers stage raids on workplaces suspected of employing undocumented aliens and take any they find into custody. Sometimes officials receive tips that certain immigrants are in the country illegally. The process can also begin with an arrest for some other crime. While performing a routine check into the background of the person under arrest, police discover that he or she is an unauthorized immigrant. The initial arrest may be for a serious crime such as assault, vehicle theft, or armed robbery. But quite often it is for a much less significant crime. Many undocumented aliens have been taken into custody because of a routine traffic stop, for example. Having a malfunctioning turn signal or a broken headlight might earn a legal resident a traffic ticket, but can lead to the arrest and eventual

43

deportation of an undocumented driver. For unauthorized aliens, a quick trip to the store in a less-than-perfect car can mean never going home again.

Though the arrest itself takes a matter of minutes, the process of deportation drags on much longer. Those suspected of being in the country illegally are entitled to due process of law; that is, they must be given a day in court and an opportunity to argue that they should be allowed to remain in the United States. But the court system moves slowly, the backlog of cases is often huge, and it can take time to gather the evidence necessary to determine whether a person is entitled to be in the country. The result is that people may wait for days, weeks, even months after being arrested until their cases are heard. Some are allowed to return home upon payment of a bond, money that will be forfeited should the immigrant fail to appear for a hearing. Most, however, cannot afford a bond or are not offered the possibility of paying it. They are kept in facilities called detention centers, and they are known as detainees.

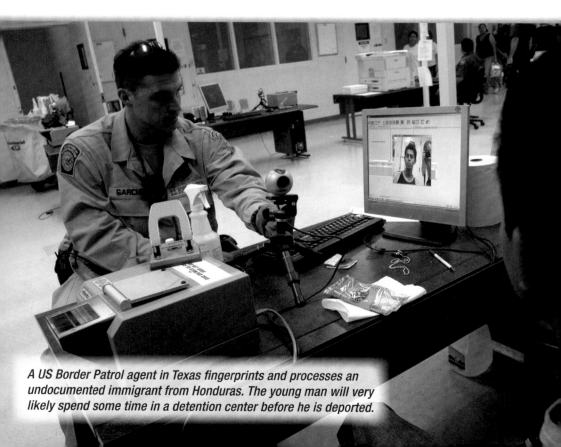

A US Border Patrol agent in Texas fingerprints and processes an undocumented immigrant from Honduras. The young man will very likely spend some time in a detention center before he is deported.

Women and Children

More than 250 sites across the United States currently serve as detention centers. Most of these are ordinary prisons and county jails built to house inmates of all descriptions and not limited to undocumented immigrants. The majority of these, in turn, house only a handful of people at any given time who are being detained for immigration issues. The bulk of immigrant detainees are housed instead at special migrant detention centers, of which there are about two dozen scattered across the United States. These vary in size. The Elizabeth Detention Center in New Jersey, for example, has a capacity of about three hundred, and the Eloy Detention Center in Eloy, Arizona, holds about five times that many. Some of these facilities are owned and operated by government agencies like ICE and the Department of Homeland Security, but others—such as Eloy—are private prisons run by for-profit companies under a government contract.

Each year an average of four hundred thousand undocumented immigrants are placed in detention centers. Though adults make up the majority of these people, the detainee population includes many younger immigrants as well. Most of these young people are taken into custody along with their mothers. Some are longtime residents of the United States; they were arrested after a raid or sent to detention following an arrest of the mother for some other infraction. Others were caught when they attempted to cross the border from Mexico or, more rarely, Canada. In the last few years, in particular, a large number of Central American women and children have traveled through Mexico in hopes of reaching the United States. All are fleeing poverty, abuse, and gang violence. Many of these mothers and children are apprehended when they try to cross the border into the United States. Others successfully cross into the country and are picked up while traveling toward towns and cities. In both cases, the family is usually sent to a detention facility equipped to handle both children and adults.

The life of a detainee in this setting is not a pleasant one. The detention centers intended for women and children are stark, cheerless places where overcrowding is frequent and mistreatment by guards is common. Those who have been kept in these

45

centers seldom have anything good to say about their detainment. Indeed, many agree with the sentiments of Yanira, a woman from Guatemala who traveled more than 1,500 miles (2,414 km) with her three children to the United States, only to be placed in a detention center when she reached the border. Asked to choose which was worse, life in the detention center or the grueling and dangerous journey north, Yanira did not hesitate. "It was definitely the detention,"[35] she says.

For women traveling with children, as Yanira did, the problem begins with the holding cells where women and children are temporarily placed when taken into custody at the border. Kathleen O'Connor, a researcher who studies Central American detainees, notes that women and children from places like El Salvador are generally put in cage-like shelters known as "the dog kennels"[36] after being apprehended. These shelters are often kept at uncomfortably low temperatures, and they typically lack beds and pillows. They are crowded, uncomfortable places, made all the more disagreeable given the length of the journeys the mothers and their children have just completed. Detainees are not supposed to be kept at these places for longer than a few days, but many wait a week or more to be transferred elsewhere.

"It's appalling how they were treated."[37]

—Professor Kathleen O'Connor on detained women and children.

The problem with holding areas goes well beyond a lack of comfort, however. O'Connor cites instances when detainees in these holding cells have been denied basic medical care and necessary personal items. Many women have said that they and their children were not permitted to bathe or even to brush their teeth. Several times O'Connor has provided items such as toothbrushes to detained women and children at her own expense. "The little necessities of life that you need," she says, "and they're just not given them or access or avenue to get them. . . . It's appalling how they were treated."[37] In a 2015 court case brought by advocates for the detainees, federal judge Dolly Gee agreed that the conditions for families

Young Adults in Eloy

Eloy, Arizona, a town about halfway between Phoenix and Tucson, is home to the Eloy Detention Center. Eloy is run by a for-profit corporation called Corrections Corporation of America. It is one of the largest of the detention centers used to house immigrants in the United States, and it is also among the most controversial. Used as a site for adults and older teenagers, Eloy is noted as a particularly unpleasant place to be. Visitors are allowed for only a few hours on the weekends, detainee phone privileges are sharply limited, and though the center is not technically considered a prison, it has the feel of one.

Eloy has made the news on several occasions because of its harsh conditions. One of these occasions took place in the summer of 2013, when a group of undocumented young adults born in Mexico but raised largely in the United States staged a protest at the Mexican border. They were arrested and taken to Eloy. "I always heard how it was horrible, humiliating," says one protester, Adriana Diaz. The rumors turned out to be true. "The clothes smelled nasty, like plastic," Diaz reports. "We hated the food. The oatmeal was an insult to oatmeal. It was like glue. It tasted disgusting." When two of Diaz's fellow detainees organized another protest in Eloy, they were put in solitary confinement. "I was seventeen days in Eloy," Diaz says today. "It felt like a year."

Quoted in Margaret Regan, *Detained and Deported*. Boston: Beacon, 2015, pp. 225–26.

in these holding areas were "deplorable." Government officials, Gee charged, "failed to meet even the minimal standard [of] safe and sanitary"[38] conditions in holding areas. Her ruling requires the government to improve conditions over time.

Detention Centers

Once children and their mothers are transferred from the holding cells to the detention centers themselves, conditions do not

Guards at a federal detention facility in New Mexico escort a young woman and her child to a waiting van. Detention facilities for undocumented immigrants are often crowded and uncomfortable.

necessarily improve. Punishment at these facilities, for example, is frequent, arbitrary, and sometimes excessive. When children misbehaved at a detention center in Artesia, New Mexico, for example, the center staff responded by revoking the telephone privileges of all inmates. At another center for family groups, this one in Karnes, Texas, several women and their children charged that they were put in solitary confinement because the women had complained about living conditions. "They were placed in a dark room," says Mohammad Abdollahi, an advocate for immigration rights. "The lights would turn on only when they were getting fed." According to Abdollahi, one of the women said to a prison guard, "You can do this to me, but why are you doing this to my child?"[39]

Health in the detention centers is another issue, especially for younger children. The water at Karnes is heavily chlorinated, and drinking it is hard on the intestinal systems of young detainees. Bottled water is available for purchase, but a single small bottle costs nearly as much as a day's pay for an inmate who holds a job in the center. The food served at Karnes, moreover, has been described by detainees as almost inedible; many children are unable to choke it down, do not get all the nutrients they need, and lose weight they should not be losing. Mothers at several detention sites have charged that staffers would not let them have cough syrup and other basic medicines for their children. And getting enough exercise can be difficult. At the Hutto Residential Center in Texas, which stopped housing families in 2009, outdoor playtime for children was limited to a single hour each day.

"You can do this to me, but why are you doing this to my child?"[39]

—A detainee punished by being placed, with her child, in a dark room.

Other issues are common as well. Women who complain about the conditions are sometimes told that they will lose custody of their children if they continue their protests. Guards at one Texas facility separated boys over the age of five from their mothers. When one woman objected that her son was too young to be kept away from her, she was told that she should "let him become a man."[40] At the same facility, roll calls were common throughout the night. Sleeping families were awakened abruptly and made to line up in front of their cells in order to be counted. Women who were slow to awaken were sometimes kicked into consciousness by the guards. The only real reason for these roll calls seemed to be to make life miserable for the detainees.

Unaccompanied Children

Not all of the children in detention are there with their mothers, however. Some Central American parents, desperate to give their children a better chance in life and unwilling or unable to travel themselves, have their children make the trek alone. They may be coming to join an aunt, a grandfather, or a parent who has already migrated to the United States, but some are simply sent north in hopes that someone will take care of them. In 2014 almost seventy thousand unaccompanied minors were apprehended by law enforcement officers. Like the family groups, some were intercepted at the Mexican border, but others were apprehended after crossing into the United States. These unaccompanied children—most at least eleven or twelve years old but some younger—are generally sent to detention settings reserved for minors.

The type and quality of these settings vary considerably. In some communities, social service departments take charge of the children and send them to foster families or group homes intended for youth. More often, they are placed in shelters intended solely for immigrant children. Still others are sent to full-fledged detention facilities, some of them as large as those meant for adults and housing dozens or even hundreds of immigrant children. In general, young people at these larger facilities are segregated by gender and age: thirteen- to fifteen-year-old boys in one section or wing of a building, for example, or ten- to twelve-year-old girls on a floor of their own. The groups may be mixed for meals, exercise, or other activities, but they spend the bulk of their time apart.

By most accounts, detention centers serving youth are more humanely run than centers for adults or for mothers and their children. "They are fed and clothed, kept clean and cool, far better off than if they were walking through the desert in June temperatures," notes reporter Michael Kiefer, observing children and teenagers at a detention site in Arizona. The staff members at these detention centers, according to Kiefer, also treated residents with kindness, unlike some of their counterparts at other facilities. "The . . . agents in the building," he writes, "seem to be genuinely compassionate in their interactions with the children."[41] The contrast between these facilities and the ones reserved for adults or for women and children can be stark.

But that does not imply that juvenile detention centers are easy places to be. The reality is that most are gloomy places

where children and teenagers are very closely monitored, are given little to do, and have scarcely any control over their lives. "The kids were never left unattended," says a researcher who visited a number of these detention sites over a four-year period. "They went to school inside [the center], they played sports inside, and they only got out for supervised outings in the community or for medical and mental-health appointments."[42] Many children find the food unfamiliar, have difficulty making friends, and desperately miss their parents. No matter how kind and attentive staff members are, life in a juvenile facility can hardly be considered normal.

Central American Refugees

Recent events, moreover, have stretched juvenile facilities to the breaking point and sometimes beyond. The tens of thousands of unaccompanied Central American children who poured into the United States in 2014, in particular, proved overwhelming. For

Asylum

Many undocumented Central Americans have arrived in the United States. In recent years those detained by border officials are generally deported as soon as possible. But some of these migrants, especially women and children traveling together and children traveling alone, have asked the US government for special consideration to enable them to stay in America. They say they are seeking asylum—that is, looking for refuge from persecution in their home countries.

The concept of asylum is nothing new. Over the years the United States has accepted many refugees from countries where persecution is common. In recent years asylum seekers have come to the United States from Bosnia and Herzegovina, Laos, and Liberia, among others. Today the United States accepts about forty-eight thousand asylum seekers every year, more than any other country.

There is no question that many Central Americans are in danger in their homelands; Honduras, for instance, has the world's highest murder rate. It can be difficult for Central Americans to establish a need for asylum, however, because simply fleeing from violence is not generally sufficient to earn refugee status. Rather, people must demonstrate that they belong to a particular social group that has been singled out for persecution. This generally means racial or religious bias, but some Central Americans have successfully argued that they fit the description because their families have been targeted for violence by drug lords or gang members. For most undocumented detainees from Central America, seeking asylum is the most likely method of getting to stay in the United States.

months, detention centers for minors were badly overcrowded. "It was very hard to sleep," a teenager at a California facility explained in the fall of 2014, "because there were so many people and not enough room to lie down."[43] Some facilities set up so many cots or mattresses so close together in sleeping quarters that moving around was almost impossible. One holding area in Texas, built to house 250 detainees, was used for twice that many. "Immigrant youths covered the dirty concrete floors," wrote a reporter, "sprawled shoulder to shoulder and draped in grubby Red Cross blankets, enveloped in a haze of sweat and body odor."[44]

Indeed, government officials were forced at the time to house children and teenagers in military bases, warehouses, and other facilities not intended for human habitation. In these places, conditions were often especially unpleasant. Residents used portable toilets, showered in trailers hastily set up on the premises, and slept on the floor. At one emergency facility in Arizona, a former warehouse that was temporarily home to as many as one thousand undocumented children and teenagers, outdoor recreation opportunities included a few Frisbees and a single basketball court. Most of the time, wrote a reporter visiting the site, the detainees sat and did nothing. The goal was to move the children to more permanent facilities as soon as possible, but the sheer number of unaccompanied detainees made this process much more difficult than it might otherwise have been.

In 2015 the number of unaccompanied minors from Central America seeking admission to the United States began to diminish, relieving some of the pressure on the juvenile detention facilities. As of early 2016 most undocumented youth detained by the US government were living in places that were built to house them. There is no guarantee, however, that the exodus of young people from Central America will not start up once again. Whether government officials will be prepared is uncertain. In the meantime, conditions for undocumented youth at detention centers, whether with their mothers or on their own, remain less than what they could be. Until problems such as overcrowding, abusive behavior by guards, and a lack of recreation opportunities are solved, that will remain the case.

> "It was very hard to sleep because there were so many people and not enough room to lie down."[43]
>
> —An undocumented teenager in detention in 2014.

Chapter 5

Efforts to Help

Fear of arrest and deportation, missing out on rites of passage, the harsh reality of detention—all of these combine to make the life of an undocumented youth difficult. To teenagers and children who are here illegally, everyone is a potential threat: police officers are viewed with suspicion, school officials are not always to be trusted, and even doctors and nurses might be better avoided. Undocumented young people, like their parents, seek to blend in, to hide in the shadows, to go about their business without being noticed, worried that someone, somehow, might discover the truth about them. That can be a hard and lonely life.

That is particularly true when undocumented families run into trouble and need assistance. Many government-based social service programs are expressly off-limits to the undocumented population. Welfare benefits, for example, are unavailable to immigrants who are here illegally; for that matter, even legal immigrants cannot qualify for welfare payments until they have been in the United States for five years. The same holds true for food stamps. Medicaid, a medical insurance program aimed at poorer Americans, also cannot be used by the undocumented in most states, and people hoping to get housing subsidies or live in public housing projects generally need to be citizens or legal immigrants as well. While an American citizen who falls upon hard times can receive government social service benefits like these, undocumented immigrants generally cannot.

Still, there are a number of organizations, both private and public, that can and do help undocumented aliens, especially teenagers and children. These groups run the gamut from government agencies permitted to give certain kinds of assistance to unauthorized migrants to privately run organizations that offer less publicized help to people in particular need. No one would say that undocumented immigrant families receive all the help they require. But the programs in place do provide a safety net of sorts to unauthorized immigrant families who are having special difficulties.

Schools

Although most government agencies cannot help undocumented children and youth, there is one major exception: the US public school system. In 1982, in a case known as *Plyler v. Doe*, the US Supreme Court ruled that undocumented children were entitled to a free public education through twelfth grade on the same basis as legal immigrants and US citizens. Like those here legally, undocumented children need to prove that they live in the district where they attend school. *Plyler* makes it clear, however, that the question of whether students are here legally is not the business of school officials. As the Department of Justice explains in a

First graders work with a teacher on sentence structure. Many of the parents of children who attend this school in Los Angeles are in the United States illegally.

document aimed at unauthorized immigrant parents, "A school district *may not* ask about your or your child's citizenship or immigration status to establish residency within the district."[45]

The ability to attend school is, of course, an enormous benefit in itself. Many children who are here illegally would have gotten little or no education in their home countries. In some cases schooling is simply unavailable or stops at a fifth- or sixth-grade level; in others, it costs more than parents can afford. In the United States, in contrast, children do have the opportunity to learn. And quite a few do exactly that; by one estimate, about sixty-five thousand undocumented teenagers graduate from US high schools every year. Though there are barriers preventing them from easily moving into the workforce, going on to college, or joining the military, the education they receive has quite a number of benefits, among them the ability to assist their parents by translating documents, explaining American ways, and navigating bureaucratic systems.

About one-third of undocumented teenagers and children live below the poverty line, moreover, and these youths benefit from free public schooling in another way. Most school districts offer lunch to their students, and sometimes breakfast as well. For impoverished students, the cost of these meals is heavily subsidized or even free of charge, depending on the family's income level. During the school year, at least, the families of these students may be able to save significant money on food, especially if they have more than one child in the school system. The children, moreover, can be sure of getting a nutritious—and hopefully filling—meal, possibly two, on a daily basis.

Health Care

Schools are probably the most important of the public benefits available to undocumented youth, but there are others. Among these is health care. Though circumstances vary considerably around the country, some state and local governments do supply health coverage at public expense for unauthorized minors. In Illinois, for example, the All Kids program is open to anyone under nineteen who meets income eligibility guidelines, despite whether they are here legally. Several states have chosen to use Medicaid funds to pro-

"Do You Have a Green Card?"

In this excerpt from his book *Undocumented*, Dan-el Padilla Peralta of New York City describes a trip to the city welfare office when he was eight years old. Padilla and his mother were undocumented Dominicans; his younger brother, however, had been born in the United States.

We had no money. Mom couldn't find a job because she had to take care of us. We were hungry.

The caseworker asked a few questions.

"Are you *ciudadanos* [citizens]? Do you have a green card?"

Mom replied, "My son Yando is a citizen. My son Dan-el and I are not."

The caseworker looked up from her desk. "Green card?"

"No.". . .

For a moment the caseworker was silent. I wondered if she was going to ask more about our *papeles* [papers], but instead she simply said, "Only your son Yando will be eligible for public assistance. . . . You will receive a fixed amount in food stamps and in cash twice a month: sixty dollars in food stamps, forty-two fifty in cash."

Mom's face turned bright red. "Is that all my son Yando is eligible for? That's not enough to feed a family!"

The caseworker shrugged. "That's all."

Dan-el Padilla Peralta, *Undocumented*. New York: Penguin, 2015, p. 20.

vide specific treatments to ailing members of the undocumented population. North Carolina and New York, for example, permit undocumented immigrant patients, including teenagers and children, to receive Medicaid-funded dialysis treatments.

Every state, moreover, has at least several health centers funded by a federal agency called the Health Resources and Services Administration. Most of these places are known as federally qualified health centers. Their mission is to provide primary medical care to anyone who shows up, regardless of their ability to pay. Nor can they turn patients away because of their immigration status. The same department also runs clinics called migrant health centers, which are available on the same basis to migrant farmworkers—nearly all of whom are immigrants, and some of whom are here without documentation. (Some migrant health centers are run instead by local or state governments.) Within the undocumented population, these health centers are perhaps especially vital for children. Young children in particular get sick on a more regular basis than adults.

Finally, there is a safety net for all undocumented aliens regardless of the state they live in or the distance from their home to a health center. By federal law, nearly all US hospitals are required to give care on an emergency basis to anyone, including those who are not legally in the country. Despite these options, many undocumented immigrants avoid seeking medical care, believing that they will be charged more than they can afford, turned away for being here illegally—or worse, reported to ICE. Arlette Lozano, a Mexican national living in California, grew up without medical care for this very reason. As a college student she was able to buy a health care policy for the first time. Still, she was reluctant to use her benefits. "There is still shame when I go to the doctor or dentist," she says. "I have to tell them I've never been there before. To explain why is very nerve-wracking."[46]

Private Charities

Though government-run organizations can be helpful to undocumented youths and adults, most of the services provided for unauthorized immigrants are done on a private basis. Many of these are charities that help all people in need without regard to immigration status. Food banks and community kitchens are common in large American cities, for instance, and in many smaller communities as well. In some parts of the country, large numbers of the people served are without documentation. Other organizations collect and distribute used clothing to people in need. Again, in places with high immigrant populations, many of the beneficiaries are undocumented aliens. Similarly, emergency housing, such as shelters for the homeless, is typically available to anyone, including immigrants without the proper papers.

In cities with large numbers of migrants, moreover, private organizations are sometimes set up to provide specifically or mainly for the needs of undocumented immigrants. In Los Angeles, a group called the Association of Raza Educators provides scholarship money for undocumented students from the city's public schools who are hoping to attend college. In Philadelphia, Puentes de Salud is a nonprofit health center where doctors routinely donate their time and expertise, allowing patients—nearly all of

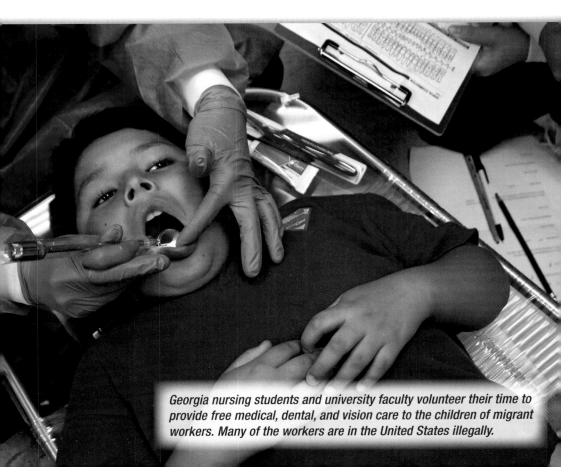

Georgia nursing students and university faculty volunteer their time to provide free medical, dental, and vision care to the children of migrant workers. Many of the workers are in the United States illegally.

them undocumented aliens—to pay fees as low as twenty dollars for a visit. "This is an underground health system,"[47] says Steve Larson, a physician who helped found the group. As Larson indicates, organizations that cater mainly to undocumented immigrants do not typically attempt to call attention to themselves. Most publicize themselves through word of mouth rather than by using standard techniques such as newspaper articles, television reports, and extensive advertising.

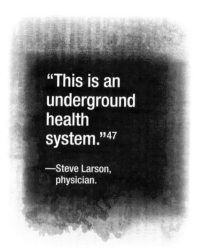

"This is an underground health system."[47]

—Steve Larson, physician.

Other organizations assist people making their way north from the Mexican border. Members of a group known as Border Angels leave gallon water jugs in places where migrants might find them as they travel through the Southwestern deserts. Water is a precious commodity in the arid wilderness, and hundreds of travelers in the region have died since 2000 for lack of it. In southern Arizona members of a group of churches offer food, temporary housing, and transportation to migrants bound for cities farther north. Organizations in other communities do the same. Hearkening back to the loose network of abolitionists that gave shelter and assistance to fugitive slaves before the Civil War, some activists have called this arrangement "a growing 21st century Underground Railroad"[48] for undocumented immigrants.

Legal Assistance

In some ways the most important form of assistance offered to undocumented aliens consists of legal advice. Living in a foreign country is difficult for anyone, and the difficulties mount exponentially for immigrants who are in the United States illegally. In particular, learning what rights undocumented aliens have and do not have is a complicated process. Undocumented immigrants often need expert help to distinguish what they are allowed to do from activities that will get them in trouble. Private attorneys are often available—their ads are easy to find on the Internet and in

A School Within a School

Undocumented immigrants who come to the United States when they are in their teens frequently have more difficulties with school than youth who come at a younger age. Very few are fluent in English when they arrive, and learning a new language can be a long and arduous process. In addition, many new arrivals have not had much formal education in their home countries, which puts them behind even in subjects like mathematics where language skills are less important. Moreover, these undocumented youths are dealing with a new country and a new culture, and it can be difficult for them to fit in socially. Some are teased or bullied; others are ignored by their peers.

As a response to these issues, several school districts nationwide have established schools specifically for recent newcomers to the United States. Most, but not all, of these students are undocumented. The District of Columbia, for example, set up the International Academy for English-Language Learners on the grounds of an existing public high school. As of 2015 this school had about two hundred enrolled students, most of them from Central American countries. Many were among the unaccompanied minors who came to the United States in 2014. Students learn English and other subjects in an environment tuned to their specific needs. "There's a lot of relationship-building before we even get to the academics," says one teacher. "It's been harder than we anticipated, but the rewards have been great, too." Another adds, "This is where they feel safe and comfortable." Some education experts expect more schools like this in the future.

Quoted in Corey Mitchell, "In U.S. Schools, Undocumented Youths Strive to Adjust," *Education Week*, May 4, 2015. www.edweek.org.

print publications—but their fees are sometimes more than low-wage immigrants can afford to pay. Accordingly, many cities and towns, especially near the Mexican border, have legal assistance clinics, staffed by lawyers, law students, and paralegals, that can provide low-cost advice to undocumented aliens in need of help.

Lawyers at these clinics act on behalf of undocumented aliens in several ways. They may advise immigrants on job-related issues, help them apply for legal status, or offer assistance when they run into trouble with the law. Whereas some of these clinics are funded by private donors and foundations, others have ties to public institutions. The University of California, for example, opened its Undocumented Legal Services Center in 2014. The legal aid offered is primarily aimed at students at various campuses in the UC system. As a professor explains, the assistance supplied "could be anything from filing to become a permanent resident, to [obtaining] a work visa—anything that relates to immigration law."[49] The University of Texas has a similar program, though its work is not limited to immigrants here illegally. Most of these clinics operate on a sliding-scale fee basis, where clients are asked to pay according to their ability.

Legal assistance is especially necessary for families that have been threatened with deportation. Staying out of custody is of critical importance for those charged with being in the country illegally. Not only do detainees lose their jobs and become separated from friends and family, but it also is easy for detainees to languish for weeks and even months before their cases are heard. The help of lawyers can be essential to keep an undocumented alien out of detention, to arrange for a bond, or to get people released from custody. In 2013, high school student Mariana Rodriguez spent several months in detention in Arizona. She was eventually released, thanks in large part to the timely assistance of a legal aid group called the Florence Immigrant and Refugee Rights Project. "These are life-and-death stakes," says Elora Mukherjee, who directs a New York immigrant rights clinic, "and it is so important to have dedicated counsel helping families through the process."[50]

Even just determining where a detainee has been taken can be difficult for an immigrant family without the help of an attorney. ICE has a tendency to shuffle detainees from one center to another, often without notifying friends and families of what is happening. It is not uncommon for someone in one state to be abruptly moved to another one 1,000 miles (1,609 km) away or more. Attorneys accustomed to how ICE operates can often help find where a detainee has been taken, though, as author Margaret Regan points out, their resourcefulness has its limits. "Sometimes even lawyers who know the system need a week or more to locate a detained client,"[51] Regan writes. Without a lawyer, it may take several weeks to identify a detainee's whereabouts, let alone begin the process of trying to set him or her free. That is especially problematic if youth are involved, such as when the detainee is a teenager or when a mother and child have been taken into custody together.

The Need for Help

A particular need for legal assistance arises when a custodial parent is placed in detention—but his or her children are not. This may happen when a child is an American citizen by virtue of having been born in the United States. It also can occur because undocumented parents take steps to hide their children from law enforcement officials. "Parents nabbed by ICE may not tell officers that they even have children," writes Regan, "for fear that the state will take their kids away from a loving aunt or grandmother or friend now caring for them."[52] If the parents are deported, caregivers often must seek expert legal help to ensure that the children can stay in a familiar place rather than being placed in foster

Lawyers provide free legal help to young people who are seeking to qualify for a federal program that would allow them to stay in the United States without fear of deportation. The program was open to youth who were brought illegally to this country before age sixteen.

care or that parental rights are not taken away altogether. This may require, for example, that a caregiver be given temporary legal guardianship of a child, something that is unlikely to be accomplished without professional assistance.

The rise in the number of unaccompanied Central American children who entered the United States in 2013 and 2014 also led to a rise in the need for legal services. With tens of thousands of young people flooding the system, it began taking months for many of their cases to be heard. As of the fall of 2015, thousands of arrivals from 2013 were still awaiting a final court date; a few had been waiting since 2011. Those who were represented by an attorney tended to have their cases heard more quickly than others, and they were also more likely to win permission to stay in the country. "Because of my attorneys' help in telling my story," says a young immigrant from Honduras who was granted judicial permission to stay in the country, "I have permanent safety in the United States."[53]

> "Because of my attorneys' help in telling my story, I have permanent safety in the United States."[53]
>
> —An undocumented Honduran immigrant.

Given this disparity and the fact that the government does not provide legal representation for these unaccompanied minors, several nonprofit organizations have sprung up in the last few years to provide free legal services for undocumented youth traveling alone. Actor Angelina Jolie, for example, teamed up with Microsoft to found a group called Kids in Need of Defense (KIND). This organization provides lawyers to help these children during their deportation proceedings. "Together," KIND's website promises, "we ensure that no child stands alone."[54] Even governments acknowledge that legal representation for these children is wise. In late 2014 the Obama administration announced a plan to provide $9 million in federal funds over a two-year period to help pay for lawyers representing unaccompanied children. The state of California, along with the city governments of San Francisco and New York City, also will provide money for legal assistance under these circumstances.

Not Alone

Immigrant families come to the United States to better their lives. Few, if any, are here for the government benefits, especially considering that aside from schools most government-based social services are not open to them. On the contrary, the bulk of immigrants hope—and expect—to make it in American society largely on their own. Still, for people who are economically, politically, and socially marginalized, the knowledge that help is available through private or public agencies can be comforting. From legal assistance to low-cost school meals, from clothing distribution centers to government-backed health care clinics, undocumented children and teenagers are not necessarily required to stand completely on their own.

Source Notes

Introduction: Youths Without Papers

1. Quoted in Margaret Regan, *Detained and Deported*. Boston: Beacon, 2015, p. 50.
2. Quoted in Regan, *Detained and Deported*, p. 46.

Chapter 1: Undocumented Immigrants

3. Quoted in Glenn Hurowitz, "Show Me a 50-Foot Wall, and I'll Show You a 51-Foot Ladder," *Grist*, November 21, 2008. http://grist.org.
4. Quoted in William A. Schwab, *The Right to DREAM*. Fayetteville: University of Arkansas Press, 2013, p. 3.
5. Quoted in William Perez and Richard Douglas Cortes, *Undocumented Latino College Students*. El Paso: LFB Scholarly, 2011, p. 54.
6. US Government Printing Office, "Porous Borders and Downstream Costs: The Cost of Illegal Immigration on State, County, and Local Governments," August 14, 2006. www.gpo.gov.
7. American Psychological Association, "Growing Up in the Shadows," *Psychology Benefits Society* (blog), November 12, 2013. http://psychologybenefits.org.

Chapter 2: Fear

8. Quoted in Eileen Truax, *Dreamers*. Boston: Beacon, 2015, p. 19.
9. Quoted in Kris Anne Bonifacio, "Undocumented Youth Struggle with Anxiety, Depression." Youth Project, January 25, 2013. www.chicago-bureau.org.
10. Quoted in Perez and Cortes, *Undocumented Latino College Students*, p. 51.
11. Kari Lydersen, "Fear & Trauma: Undocumented Immigrants and Mental Health," Institute for Justice & Journalism, April 24, 2013. http://justicejournalism.org.

12. Luis H. Zayas, *Forgotten Citizens*. New York: Oxford University Press, 2015, p. 9.
13. Quoted in Lydersen, "Fear & Trauma."
14. Quoted in Joanna Dreby, "Executive Action on Immigration Will Help Children and Families," Center for American Progress, March 3, 2015. www.americanprogress.org.
15. Lydersen, "Fear & Trauma."
16. Jose Antonio Vargas, "My Life as an Undocumented Immigrant," *New York Times*, June 22, 2011. www.nytimes.com.
17. Quoted in Truax, *Dreamers*, pp. 19–20.
18. Quoted in Truax, *Dreamers*, p. 115.
19. Quoted in Truax, *Dreamers*, p. 28.
20. Quoted in Regan, *Detained and Deported*, p. 80.
21. Quoted in Kara B. Cebulko, *Documented, Undocumented, and Something Else: The Incorporation of Children of Brazilian Immigrants*. El Paso: LFB Scholarly, 2013, p. 67.
22. Quoted in Schwab, *The Right to DREAM*, p. 112.
23. Quoted in Truax, *Dreamers*, p. 111.
24. PBS Kids, "Immigration: Living Undocumented." http://pbskids.org.
25. Quoted in Schwab, *The Right to DREAM*, p. 114.
26. Vargas, "My Life as an Undocumented Immigrant."
27. Quoted in Regan, *Detained and Deported*, p. 224.

Chapter 3: Rites of Passage

28. Vargas, "My Life as an Undocumented Immigrant."
29. Quoted in Schwab, *The Right to DREAM*, p. 4.
30. Quoted in Gosia Woznackia, "Driver's Licenses for Undocumented Immigrants Could Be a Big Benefit of DACA in California," *Huffington Post*, September 16, 2012. www.huffingtonpost.com.
31. Quoted in Cebulko, *Documented, Undocumented, and Something Else*, p. 66.
32. Quoted in Cebulko, *Documented, Undocumented, and Something Else*, p. 125.
33. Quoted in Truax, *Dreamers*, p. 33.

34. Quoted in Lisa D. Garcia, *Undocumented and Unwanted*. El Paso: LFB Scholarly, 2013, p. 65.

Chapter 4: Detention

35. Quoted in Esther Yu-Hsi Lee, "How Immigration Detention Centers Retraumatize Women and Children Fleeing from Violence," ThinkProgress, October 22, 2015. http://think progress.org.
36. Quoted in Lee, "How Immigration Detention Centers Retraumatize Women and Children Fleeing from Violence."
37. Quoted in Lee, "How Immigration Detention Centers Retraumatize Women and Children Fleeing from Violence."
38. Quoted in Cindy Carcamo, "Judge Blasts ICE, Says Immigrant Children, Parents in Detention Centers Should Be Released," *Los Angeles Times*, July 25, 2015. www.latimes.com.
39. Quoted in Esther Yu-Hsi Lee, "Mothers and Children Allegedly Locked in a Dark Room for Protesting Detention Conditions," ThinkProgress, April 5, 2015. http://thinkprogress.org.
40. Quoted in Jocelyn Dyer and Sandra Lopez, "Families Report Abuse in Border Patrol Detention Facilities, Despite Court Ruling," Human Rights First Blog, December 1, 2015. www .humanrightsfirst.org.
41. Michael Kiefer, "First Peek: Immigrant Children Flood Detention Center," AZCentral, June 19, 2014. www.azcentral.com.
42. Quoted in Ian Gordon, "70,000 Kids Will Show Up Alone at Our Border This Year. What Happens to Them?," *Mother Jones*, July/August 2014. www.motherjones.com.
43. Quoted in Center for Human Rights and Constitutional Law, "Detention Centers." http://immigrantchildren.org.
44. Molly Hennessy-Fiske and Cindy Carcamo, "Overcrowded, Unsanitary Conditions Seen at Immigrant Detention Centers," *Los Angeles Times*, June 18, 2014. www.latimes.com.

Chapter 5: Efforts to Help

45. US Department of Justice, "Fact Sheet: Information on the Rights of All Children to Enroll in School." www.justice.gov.

46. Quoted in Lisa Zamosky, "Healthcare Options for Undocumented Immigrants," *Los Angeles Times*, April 27, 2014. www.latimes.com.
47. Quoted in Griselda Nevarez, "Undocumented Immigrants Face Limited Health Care Options," Huffington Post, January 28, 2014.
48. Quoted in Courtney E. Martin, "The Other Face of Illegal Immigration," NPR, June 29, 2011. www.npr.org.
49. Quoted in Bea Karnes, "Undocumented UC Students to Receive Free Legal Services." Patch, November 21, 2014. http://patch.com.
50. Quoted in Jazmine Ulloa, "Duo from Immigration Clinic Plays Key Role at Detention Centers," *San Angelo Standard-Times*, February 13, 2016. www.gosanangelo.com.
51. Regan, *Detained and Deported*, p. 9.
52. Regan, *Detained and Deported*, p. 119.
53. Quoted in Corporate Pro Bono, "Kids in Need of Defense (KIND)." www.cpbo.org.
54. Kids in Need of Defense, "Who We Are." https://supportkind .org.

American Psychological Association (APA)

750 First St. NE
Washington, DC 20002-4242
phone: (800) 374-2721
website: www.apa.org

The APA deals with many psychological topics, among them the effects of being undocumented on mental health. Its general position is that undocumented youth should not be made to feel bad or afraid about their status.

Dream Resource Center

UCLA Downtown Labor Center
675 S. Park View St.
Los Angeles, CA 90057-3306
phone: (213) 480-4155 ext. 220
e-mail: healthforall@irle.ucla.edu
website: http://undocumentedanduninsured.org

This California-based organization focuses on the health needs of undocumented immigrants, including youth. It seeks to provide health care and health care coverage for undocumented aliens, who generally are not eligible for health care subsidies.

Florida Immigrant Coalition

website: https://floridaimmigrant.org

The Florida Immigrant Coalition lobbies for the rights of undocumented immigrants, including students. It works for immigration reform, helps immigrants find legal assistance, and serves as a clearinghouse for news items of interest to undocumented aliens.

Immigrant Youth Justice League (IYJL)

4753 N. Broadway, Suite 904
Chicago, IL 60640
website: www.iyjl.org
e-mail: info@iyjl.org

The IYJL is a Chicago-based group led primarily by young undocumented immigrants. It provides assistance to those here illegally and works to change American policy regarding undocumented aliens.

International Institute of Akron (IIA)

207 E. Tallmadge Ave.
Akron, OH 44310
phone: (330) 376-5106
website: http://iiakron.org

The IIA provides various services for undocumented aliens in northeastern Ohio, especially young people. It helps undocumented youth obtain work authorizations and visas and offers legal representation for those facing deportation.

Kids in Need of Defense (KIND)

1300 L St. NW, Suite 1100
Washington, DC 20005
phone: (202) 824-8680
e-mail: info@supportkind.org
website: https://supportkind.org

KIND, founded in part by actor Angelina Jolie and Microsoft, provides legal assistance to undocumented children, especially those who arrive at the US border without being accompanied by adults.

United We Dream (UWD)

1900 L St. NW, Suite 900
Washington DC 20036
website: http://unitedwedream.org

The UWD is made up primarily of undocumented young people. It advocates for the dignity and fair treatment of all immigrants, documented or not; it takes a particular interest in attempting to stop deportations and keeping families together.

Books

Lisa D. Garcia, *Undocumented and Unwanted*. El Paso: LFB Scholarly, 2013.

Margaret Regan, *Detained and Deported*. Boston: Beacon, 2015.

William A. Schwab, *The Right to DREAM*. Fayetteville: University of Arkansas Press, 2013.

Eileen Truax, *Dreamers.* Boston: Beacon, 2015.

Internet Sources

American Psychological Association, "Growing Up in the Shadows," *Psychology Benefits Society* (blog), November 12, 2013. http://psychologybenefits.org/2013/11/12/growing-up-in-the -shadows-how-unauthorized-status-puts-immigrant-youth-at-risk.

American Psychological Association, "Undocumented Americans." www.apa.org/topics/immigration/undocumented-video.aspx.

Melinda D. Anderson, "How Fears of Deportation Harm Kids' Education." *Atlantic*, January 26, 2016. www.theatlantic.com /education/archive/2016/01/the-educational-and-emotional-toll -of-deportation/426987.

Cindy Carcamo, "Judge Blasts ICE, Says Immigrant Children, Parents in Detention Centers Should Be Released," *Los Angeles Times*, July 25, 2015. www.latimes.com/local/lanow/la-me -ln-judge-orders-release-of-immigrant-children-mothers-from -detention-centers-20150725-story.html.

Ian Gordon, "70,000 Kids Will Show Up Alone at Our Border This Year. What Happens to Them?," *Mother Jones*, July/August 2014. www.motherjones.com/politics/2014/06/child-migrants-surge -unaccompanied-central-america.

Law Help NY, "Know Your Rights: Rights of Undocumented Immigrants." www.lawhelpny.org/issues/immigrationimmigrants/rights-of-immigrant-children-teenagers-1?channel=know-your-rights&category=i-am-undocumented-what-rights-do-i-have&location=all.

Pew Research Center, "Children 12 and Under Are Fastest Growing Group of Unaccompanied Minors at U.S. Border." www.pewresearch.org/fact-tank/2014/07/22/children-12-and-under-are-fastest-growing-group-of-unaccompanied-minors-at-u-s-border.

Jose Antonio Vargas, "My Life as an Undocumented Immigrant," *New York Times*, June 22, 2011. www.nytimes.com/2011/06/26/magazine/my-life-as-an-undocumented-immigrant.html?_r=0.

Index

Picture Credits

About the Author

Stephen Currie has written many books for young adults and children. His work for ReferencePoint Press includes *Women World Leaders*, *Goblins*, and *Medieval Punishment and Torture*. He has also taught levels ranging from kindergarten to college. He lives in New York's Hudson Valley.